Science Tools

MICROSCOPES AND HAND LENSES

by Lisa J. Amstutz

PEBBLE
a capstone imprint

Little Pebble is published by Pebble
1710 Roe Crest Drive
North Mankato, Minnesota 56003
www.mycapstone.com

Library of Congress Cataloging-in-Publication Data is available on the Library of Congress website.
ISBN 978-1-9771-0060-3 (library binding)
ISBN 978-1-9771-0064-1 (paperback)
ISBN 978-1-9771-0068-9 (ebook pdf)

Editorial Credits
Anna Butzer, editor; Cynthia Della-Rovere, designer;
Kelly Garvin, media researcher; Tori Abraham, production specialist

Image Credits
Capstone Press/Karon Dubke, cover, 1 (top left), 15, 19, 21; iStockphoto: FatCamera, 5,17, JLBarranco, 9; Shutterstock: Dargon Images, 11, Galileo30, 1 (bottom right), Nenad Zivkovic, 3, Purino, 7, Triff, 13
Design elements: Shutterstock: Alina G, Astarina, Fafarumba, happy_fox_art, Lorelyn Medina, mhatzapa, Netkoff, Nikitina Karina, olllikeballoon, PedroNevesDesign, Visual Generation

Note to Parents and Teachers
The Science Tools set supports national standards for mathematical practice related to measurement and data. This book describes and illustrates how to use microscopes and hand lenses for observation. The images support early readers in understanding the text. The repetition of words and phrases helps early readers learn new words. This book also introduces early readers to subject-specific vocabulary words, which are defined in the Glossary section. Early readers may need assistance to read some words and to use the Table of Contents, Glossary, Read More, Internet Sites, and Index sections of the book.

All internet sites appearing in back matter were available and accurate when this book was sent to press.

Printed and bound in China.
001654

Table of Contents

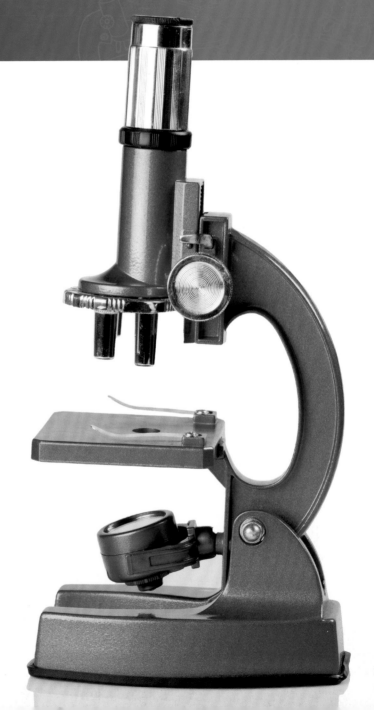

Look Closer

The world is full of tiny things. Some are too small for our eyes to see. A microscope or hand lens can help!

A lens is a curved piece
of glass. It bends light.
When you look through a lens,
a thing looks bigger than it is.

WHAT IS A HAND LENS?

A hand lens is small and easy to carry. You can put it in a backpack to take with you. Let's go explore!

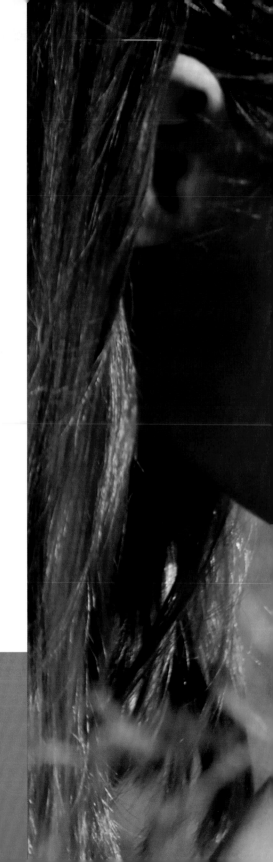

A hand lens makes things look up to 20 times bigger. Find a leaf or flower. Hold the hand lens close to your eye. Bring the leaf toward the lens.

What Is a Microscope?

A microscope has a
lens tube with two lenses.
The lens you look through
is called the eyepiece. The other
lens is called the objective.

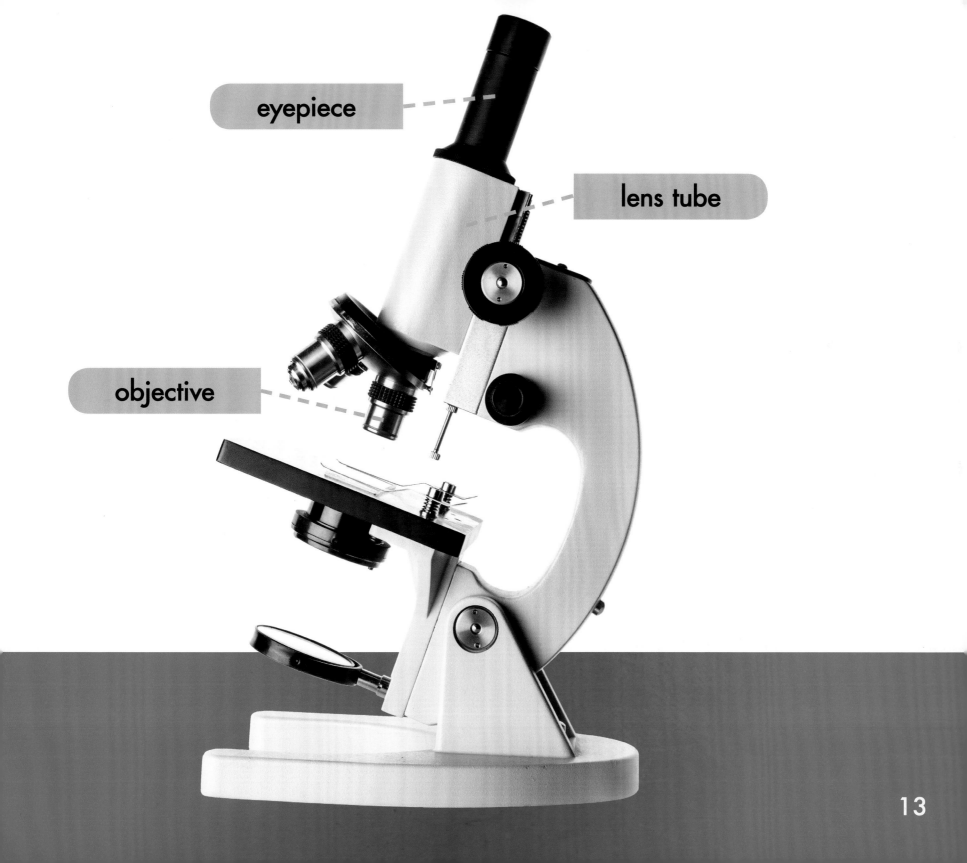

eyepiece

lens tube

objective

13

A microscope can magnify
up to 1,500 times. Place a piece
of hair on a slide. Put a slide
cover on top. Then clip the slide
onto the stage.

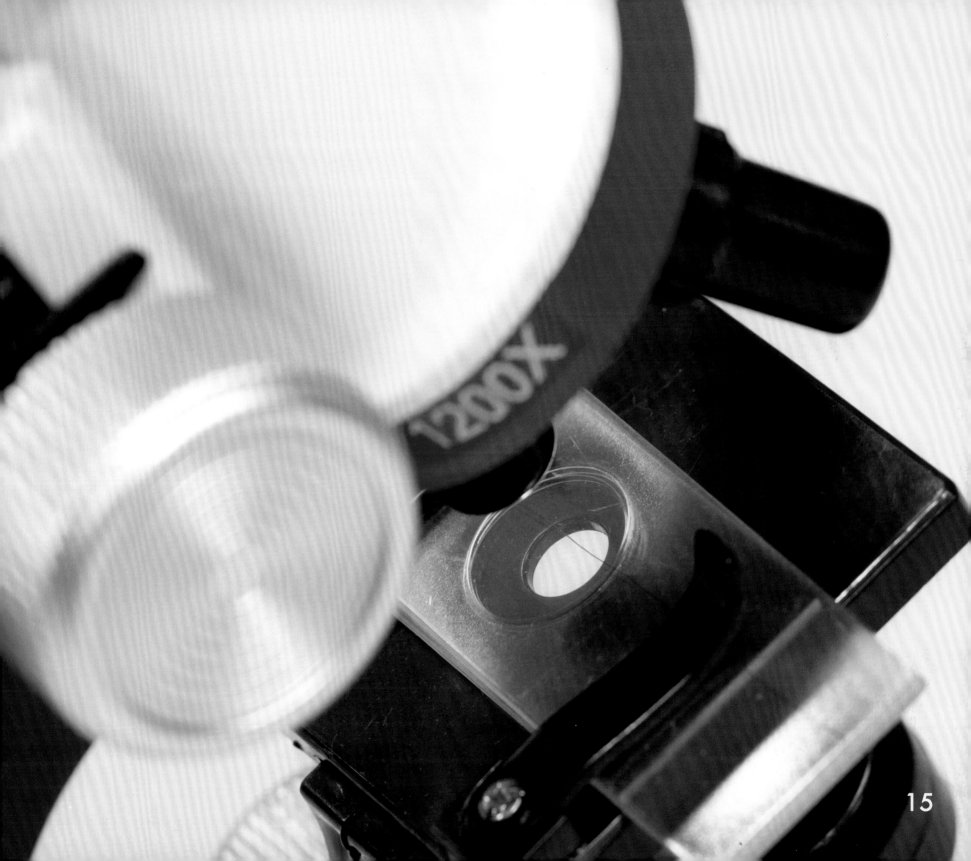

Look into the tube to see the hair. Two knobs focus the microscope. They move the lens tube up and down. Another knob moves the stage.

Safety First!

Many lenses are made of glass. They can break easily. Use both hands to pick up a microscope. Put one hand under the base. That way you will not drop it.

Microscopes and hand lenses help scientists study things closely. What new things can you discover with a lens?

GLOSSARY

base—the lowest part of something, or the part that it stands on

eyepiece—a curved piece of glass in a microscope that magnifies an image from the objective lens

focus—to bring rays of light or other energy to a point to make a clear image

magnify—to make something look larger than it really is

objective lens—a curved piece of glass in a microscope that collects light and magnifies an image

slide—a small piece of glass that holds an object so it can be seen under a microscope

stage—a platform on a microscope that holds a slide

Read More

Lopez, Max. *How Do Microscopes Work?* Infomax Common Core Readers. New York: Rosen Classroom, 2014.

Metz, Lorijo. *Using Hand Lenses and Microscopes.* Science Tools. New York: PowerKids Press, 2013.

Nelson, Maria. *Cells Up Close.* Under the Microscope. New York: Gareth Stevens Publishing, 2014.

Internet Sites

Easy Science for Kids: All About Microscopes
https://easyscienceforkids.com/all-about-microscopes/

PBS: Magnification Observation
https://pbskids.org/video/sid-science-kid/1568578354

Index